Design   David West
                            Children's Book Design
Editor   Jen Green
Picture researcher   Cecilia Weston-Baker

The author, Margaret Fagan, is a practicing psychotherapist who has edited many books on social issues.

The consultant, Jenny Morris, was a lecturer in housing policy for many years and is now a freelance writer and consultant.

First published in
the United States in 1990 by
Gloucester Press
387 Park Avenue South
New York NY 10016

Printed in Belgium

The publishers wish to acknowledge that the photographs reproduced in this book have been posed by models or obtained from photographic agencies.

Library of Congress Cataloging-in-Publication Data

Fagan, Margaret, 1955-
    The fight against homelessness / Margaret Fagan.
       p. cm. -- (Understanding social issues)
    Summary: Examines the rising social cost of
homelessness, those who are most vulnerable, and their
experiences.
    ISBN 0-531-17251-1
    1. Homelessness--Juvenile literature. [1. Homelessness.]
I.Title. II. Series.
HV4493.F34 1990
362.5--dc20   90-3214   CIP   AC

CONTENTS

UNDERSTANDING SOCIAL ISSUES

THE FIGHT AGAINST HOMELESSNESS

Margaret Fagan

GLOUCESTER PRESS
London : New York : Toronto : Sydney

The streets of the inner cities are home to thousands of people – some of them young, others in severe states of mental and physical ill health. In Britain there is a crisis of homelessness and in the United States the problem of up to three million homeless people has transformed city life.

Reactions to the problem are twofold; everyone is appalled by the plight of the homeless, but also intimidated by those homeless people with drug or alcohol problems. Some worry that these people are a new alienated, unemployable, and uneducated "underclass," who *choose* to live on the edge of society. But the homeless are on the streets or in temporary accommodation because of misfortune. They have suffered the breakdown of a relationship, or a series of setbacks. Most say of life on the street that they wouldn't wish it even on their worst enemy, that they would move on if they could, but poverty prevents them from doing so.

Concern about homelessness in industrialized nations and the Third World is growing. In the Third World poverty leads to destitution, slums, and ill health; in the inner city its effects are similar.

This book is primarily about homelessness in the affluent industrialized world: it concentrates on the conditions and experiences of both the single homeless and of homeless households. It looks only briefly at the situation in Third World countries, and it does not cover the plight of people made homeless as refugees from war or from political persecution.

Every night thousands of people camp on the streets in makeshift cardboard cities, or wherever doorways, subways, railroad stations, bridges or underground parking lots provide shelter.

CHAPTER 1
BEING
HOMELESS

People are
homeless to
different degrees:
some live in
slums like this
one in Mexico.
WHO (the World
Health
Organization)
estimates "one
quarter of the
world's
population" lives
in conditions
which directly
cause death and
disease.

In the industrialized countries the homeless problem is widening to include a broader social mix of people. In the United States, where the homeless population has doubled every year since 1980, there are now many more homeless families with children, and the average age of homeless people (34) is lower than previously. Many families who become homeless haven't the resources to rehouse themselves – they can't afford commercial rents. Social housing (low-income housing) offers a solution, but there just isn't enough to meet demand.

As the numbers of homeless people grow, it's clear that the problem is caused by changing social and political attitudes, and not by a handful of crazy or lazy people individually choosing to live on the street. In the United States the problems of the very poor are worsening – unemployment and poverty are at their worst since the Depression. In Britain there is alarm that the homeless problem will follow the same trends as in the United States.

Who is homeless in the industrialized world?
Most visible are the "roofless," those with nowhere fixed to stay, who sleep in different places every night and who are destitute. Others are squatters in derelict buildings. Some live in so-called welfare hostels, temporary accommodations provided by the authorities or local and federal government. In addition there are the "hidden homeless" – people forced to tolerate difficult living conditions to avoid being homeless. They might share an overcrowded apartment with their family or friends, or continue to be the victims of physical or sexual abuse in the home because they haven't anywhere

else to live. The "hidden" homeless, both single people and families, live under extreme psychological stress.

> **"I've been married for nine years – every one of them hell. People used to say, she must like it or she'd divorce him. In the end I left for the kids' sake – I didn't want them growing up seeing their mother treated like that."** Irene, who is staying in a shelter for battered women.

People living in residential care are also a significant number of the "hidden homeless." These people – particularly those with physical

Without an address, no one is entitled to welfare. So many of those camping on the streets in the United States, like this woman, beg for survival.

LEARNING RESOURCES CENTER
UNIVERSITY OF WYOMING LIBRARIES
LARAMIE, WY 82071

disabilities – endure unsuitable residential homes because they have no alternative. Most would prefer a home of their own.

Immediate causes of homelessness
According to official views in both the United States and Britain the most common cause of homelessness is the "unwanted guest," who gets asked to leave once friends or relatives stop offering accommodation.

> **"My son and grandson came to stay with me after their house burned down. His wife and two daughters have gone off to stay with her new boyfriend – things were already bad in the family, even before the fire. I don't want them staying here, but what can I do?"** June, aged 55.

But explaining homelessness as the failure of sharing arrangements obscures the real reasons for the problem. Behind the statistics are events or crises which force people to share – out of necessity, not choice. Breakdown of relationships, particularly marriages or partnerships, falling behind with the rent or with mortgage payments are potentially all original causes of homelessness.

In the United States further stresses are caused by programs of inner city housing renovation. One report published in 1982 claimed that about 2.5 million Americans lost their homes every year due to renovation, redevelopment, or rent increases. Most of them find alternative accommodation eventually, but many don't, joining the thousands of others made homeless by demolition, inflation, and arson. The major victims of mass development are the poor, with fewest resources to absorb new hardship.

How many people?
No one knows for sure how many people are homeless; the lack of accurate figures reflects the low priority given to the plight of the homeless. In the United States there are no official statistics, but the National Coalition for the Homeless has estimated that there were 2.5 million homeless in 1983, an increase of 500,000 over 1982. Others say the real figure is as high as 3 million. New York has the largest homeless population in the United States; the *New York Times* labeled it the "New Calcutta" and criticized the city administration's policies on homelessness.

It is estimated that there are between 70,000 and 90,000 homeless men, women, and children in New York. About 30,000 of these live in shelters which are financed either by the city or by charities usually associated with churches and synagogues. The rest live on the street in subways or derelict buildings, or at railroad and bus stations. Many of those living in New York's shelters and hotels for the homeless are children – one report claims they house 15,000 children whose average age is six. Of those on the street, 20,000 are children or teenagers. According to a report issued in 1990 by the National Commission on Children, 100,000 children are homeless throughout the United States, but advocates of homeless people consider this figure to be a wild underestimate.

In Britain and the United States there is a shortage of money to repair or improve existing housing. The block of council apartments in London where this girl lives is in urgent need of modernization.

The United States census

In 1990, in order to get a better grasp of the numbers who are homeless, the United States Census Bureau attempted to count them. The census, which is undertaken every ten years and aims to find out more about the American population of more than 250 million, had previously ignored the homeless in its count. For the 1990 census, the bureau employed 15,000 volunteers to visit 22,000 sites overnight to help take what it called "a snapshot of the homeless."

The fight against homelessness

The U.S. census has raised a lot of controversy. Some people are worried that inevitably the homeless will be undercounted, especially the most elusive group – the many thousands who sleep on the street. The head of one shelter in Washington barred census-takers from his 1,400-bed shelter and dumped a truckload of sand outside the Commerce Department in protest. He said, "It is as hard to count the homeless as it is to count these grains." Many advocates of the homeless share his view; they are concerned that an undercount could help President Bush to minimize the issue and so affect the amount of aid given to local governments to spend in the fight against homelessness.

Homeless in Britain
In Britain the definition of homelessness is a matter of debate. People on the street without a roof over their heads are clearly homeless, but they are not included in the official statistics. For the authorities the working definition of "homeless" covers only those whom they have a legal duty to accommodate. In an attempt to rehouse those in most need, the authorities accept responsibility for families with children, in which the woman is pregnant or in which persons are at risk because of old age, disability or illness. Even within these narrow definitions the authorities acutely lack the resources to satisfactorily accommodate everyone who approaches them.

Usually authorities have no legal responsibility to find accommodation for families they consider to be intentionally homeless, or for single people. In 1989 there were approximately 140,000 households (families) accepted by the local authorities as being without a home.

Although there are no national statistics for the numbers of single people who are homeless in Britain, no one disputes that the number must run into tens of thousands; one charity estimates two million. In London there are approximately 50,000 young homeless people between the ages of 16 and 19 either living on the streets, in shelters, or in abandoned buildings, according to a survey by a housing charity, Centrepoint, which provides temporary hostels for young people. There are between two and three thousand people camping on the streets of London. The size of the problem is staggering.

Why is the situation getting worse?
Even without accurate figures, everyone agrees that the number of homeless people is rising in industrialized countries in the West. Most agree about the main factors which contribute to homelessness: poverty and the lack of affordable housing due to changes in housing policies. Whatever the immediate reason for becoming homeless, once the situation has arisen, many people are too poor to solve their situation without help.

Many people are poor because of unemployment. But being employed doesn't necessarily protect people from experiencing homelessness. In New York about one fourth of homeless adults are employed. They may earn up to $200 a week but this isn't enough to pay the rent. Sometimes people share a place with friends or relatives so they can afford the rent, but this type of overcrowded situation frequently becomes strained and is a first step to a person becoming completely homeless. In New York, where rents are extremely high, 100,000 families live doubled or tripled up.

> "It was like being on a treadmill – no matter how hard he worked, he didn't earn enough. At one point he was working all days and some nights to pay the rent and keep up the payments on the furniture we'd bought. In the end we fell behind and the landlord threw us out." Susan, now living in a cheap hotel.

Housing policies
In both Britain and the United States, as a result of government policies, there has been a decline in the number of the privately owned houses to rent, and people have been encouraged to buy their own homes. Owner occupancy is now the way most people have the secure rights to where they live (tenure), whereas 90 years ago, the private rented sector (renting from private landlords) was usual. However, it is financially more difficult to become an owner-occupier today than it was to pay low rents. Most of the housing in the private rented sector is now aimed at people with high incomes.

To make matters worse, in Britain and the United States there has also been a drastic cutback in social housing – housing built with public money and intended to be let for controlled rents to people with lower incomes. So many of the households who would have previously been private tenants can't find rented accommodation which they can afford. In the United States, the cutback in housing built for people with low incomes is almost total.

In Britain the shortage of affordable housing is made even more acute because of government policy; local authorities (councils) who provide most of the houses or apartments to rent have had to sell off their housing stock at a discount to those occupiers who can afford to buy.

The situation in the private housing sector has also tightened. Recently house prices have spiraled, and because of high interest rates, mortgages have risen too. Some house owners can no longer meet their mortgage payments and run the risk of their homes being repossessed. Because of the shortage of low-income housing, this has put added pressure on the housing market.

Since the earthquake in Armenia destroyed their homes, thousands of people have had to live in temporary accommodation until they are rehoused.

Single-room occupancy
In the United States single-room occupancy (SRO) hotels were once the mainstay of housing for the very poor, the elderly and those discharged from psychiatric hospitals (see chapter 4). These "hotels," owned by private landlords and often in appalling condition, charged rents affordable to low-income earners and those receiving welfare. But in recent years most of these hotels have been demolished or converted to make way for housing for people with higher incomes. The residents of SROs were evicted without notice, but their welfare checks were not enough to cover the cost of renting alternative accommodation. About *one million* people, *most* of those who are homeless in the United States today, were turned out on the streets from SROs. In New York City alone, SROs once provided 100,000 rooms for a rent of about $200-400 a month. When this housing, deemed to be substandard, was demolished or upgraded, the 100,000 occupants became homeless.

"Places where you could live a sort of existence on a small amount of money don't really exist anymore. They pulled them down because they were so bad. They didn't put much back in their place and they were certainly better than nothing." Barry, who sleeps on the street, but used to stay in a SRO.

Closing shelters
In Britain today there are more single homeless people than ever before, yet there are fewer shelter accommodations available. Sometimes old-style

shelters were closed because better ones were planned, but then funds were not made available to build replacements. In London during the last ten years, 5,000 beds in "direct access" shelters (places that offer accommodations to people walking in off the street) have been lost.

Social housing in Germany and France
Most of West Germany's social housing, mainly apartments, was built after the end of World War II. These apartments, built with government subsidies, are available at low rent to families with many children, the disabled, old people and those with low incomes.

In Germany and France, and other European countries, most people used to live in rented accommodation, usually privately owned. However, the number of people owning their own homes has increased, and the building of new social housing has slowed. Growing numbers of young couples, large families, low-income earners, pensioners, people with disabilities and especially foreign workers can't find suitable accommodation which they can afford. In France, shantytowns have grown up outside major cities such as Paris, Lyon and Marseilles, where many migrant workers live.

Homelessness in other parts of the world
In the Third World the twin problems of poverty and the lack of affordable housing are very acute. In countries with high inflation such as Brazil, housing is a severe problem. On the outskirts of any city is the shantytown where the poorest

residents live. Again, many people have jobs, but their wages are too low to cover the rent. Some parents, too poor to look after their children, leave them on the street to fend for themselves by thieving or begging. Many sniff glue and gasoline to dull the pain of hunger and cold.

> **"We washed cars and collected scrap paper to earn money. Sometimes we shoplifted. We wanted to go to school but our clothes were ragged and we didn't have any shoes, only rubber sandals, so the teacher didn't want us. Then they let us go, but we had to sit in a corner, and we were not allowed to use the library because they said we would steal the books."** Brazilian boy.

The street children of Brazil who live in poverty and misery are constantly hassled and pursued by the police. Death squads and gangs, which include members of the police, patrol the streets and murder homeless children; in 1989 they murdered at least one child a day. Extermination is their brutal "answer" to homelessness.

Becoming homeless due to natural disaster

In some parts of the world natural disasters add to the problems of poor people. Sudden storms, for example the floods that devastated whole regions of Bangladesh in 1988, can render thousands of people homeless within days. In 1989 a severe earthquake in the Soviet republic of Armenia claimed thousands of lives. Buildings crumbled which hadn't been designed to withstand earthquakes, even though this is a region where they are common. Most of the area has been demolished for safety and a massive program of rebuilding has begun.

In San Francisco, the recent earthquake also led to loss of life and damage to many homes. But there the destruction was less and did not result in thousands of people being made homeless, partly because buildings had been properly constructed to withstand earthquakes, and partly because the people affected could afford to repair their homes.

Failure of the rains, combined with the traumatic effects of civil war, have made many thousands of people homeless in Ethiopia as they move from their homes to try to escape starvation. They have moved into camps and are dependent on international aid for survival. Although these camps were founded in response to an acute situation, many people remain there for years; children are born there and they themselves may have children there also, so remote is the chance of a settlement of the civil war or the necessary government help which would allow them to reestablish their farms.

Eastern Europe

Officially there is no such thing as homelessness in Eastern Europe. However, "doubling" is extensive in all the major cities. Most people live in apartments with very little space. Nevertheless several members of the extended family will squeeze into two or three rooms. Perhaps the grandparents may live in one room, the husband and wife in another, while the children share a third room. Rooms are used for more than one purpose; the mother and father's bedroom may serve as the sitting room or dining room during the day.

South Africa

Outside the major cities in South Africa are the sprawling townships that are home to millions of black people. Because of the laws of apartheid, they are forced to live away from the towns where they work. These laws (the Group Areas Act) insist that white and black people do not live in the same areas, but are racially segregated. Soweto, outside Johannesburg, is probably the best known of these. Many townships started as illegal squats or shantytowns and still, today, do not have essential basic facilities such as sewage systems and street lighting. Some shantytowns such as Crossroads outside Cape Town still remain. There conditions are at their worst: the inhabitants have no legal rights to their "homes," often made of cardboard or bits of corrugated iron, since the shantytowns have grown up in defiance of the Group Areas Act. Crossroads has been bulldozed by security forces several times, only to grow up again.

About 12 million black Africans live in the so-called homelands, tracts of poor land which have been made over to the black population and are allegedly independent. Some families live there while the men work in the major towns within South Africa itself. But those who have jobs object to living in this way – it divides families often for long periods of time, since the homelands are far away from the major towns. However, most of the people who live there are unemployed.

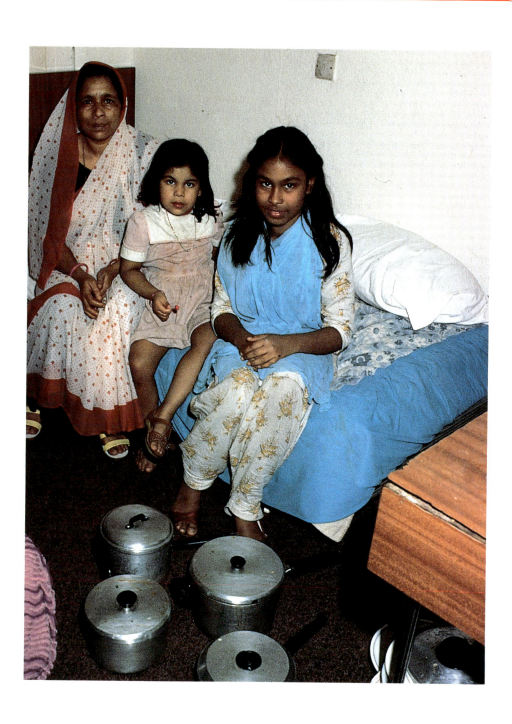

CHAPTER 2

HOMELESS FAMILIES

Homeless families in shelters are forced to live in cramped conditions. Those families who are at greatest risk of becoming homeless in connection with poverty are single parents, ethnic minorities and the unemployed.

Families are a large proportion of the homeless people in Western cities. In Britain over the past ten years over a million households have been accepted by local authorities as homeless; that means 3 million people altogether, with 1.4 million dependent children. The substantial majority (80 to 85 percent) of households accepted as homeless by local authorities are either families with young children or ones in which the woman is pregnant. Yet the actual number of homeless families is even greater. More families apply to local authorities but are not officially classed as homeless. Others do not even bother – they suspect it would be a waste of time.

In the United States, families, mainly single women with children, make up 21 percent of the homeless population, and they are the fastest growing group among the homeless. They are also the group most affected by the scarcity of low-income housing, and have been increasingly hit by inflation and the rising cost of essentials such as electricity and food. The figure of 100,000 homeless families in 1989 is almost certainly an underestimate.

The "hotel" homeless

In Britain, because of the housing shortage, local authorities provide temporary accommodation for those they accept as homeless in "bed and breakfast" hotels. These places offer poor facilities and specifically cater to the homeless. Many are substandard, most are expensive. Despite the fact that families are supposed to be there on a short-term basis, they end up staying for periods of up to three years. The poor condition of such places is well known but, with no alternatives available, they continue to be used. In fact more money is paid to the owners in rent than it costs to build new low-income housing.

Living in hotels and motels

In the United States, homeless families are housed by some city administrations in subsidized hotels and motels (welfare hotels). Provision varies from state to state; some have increased their spending to help, but the national trend is to cut back. New York City has the most extensive provision.

So long as the federal government remains committed to the provision of temporary shelter, rather than low-income housing, the situation for homeless families can only get worse. In 1985 there were 1.9 million privately owned, federally subsidized housing units – all of which had been built with government incentives in the 1960s. As the original financing contracts have expired, many units have been taken out of the low-income pool by their private owners and no new low-income housing has been added. Consequently, the stock of public housing in the United States is declining and what is left is in serious disrepair. Families who are housed in hotels and motels cannot realistically expect to find alternatives.

Cities such as New York spend their funds for emergency shelter on paying exorbitant rents to private landlords who make huge profits. The city also provides a "restaurant" allowance so that the estimated 3,000 people living in welfare hotels, which usually don't provide any cooking facilities, can eat in cheap restaurants or buy a meal at one of the city shelters. More money is spent on housing homeless families in hotels than would be spent on renting luxury apartments for them.

Bad housing is harmful to a family's health – both mental and physical. "The connection between health and dwellings of the population is one of the most important that exists," said Florence Nightingale, a Victorian nurse. Homeless people are still waiting for change.

Families in rural areas

Homeless families are in dire poverty and not only in the inner cities. Poverty and unemployment often hit hardest in rural areas – in today's rural America one child in four lives below the poverty line, compared with one in five in the cities. In Britain, rural areas and the provincial cities are areas of high unemployment, and about 40 percent of households accepted as homeless live outside the big towns and cities.

The "new poor" are the bread-winners of families who have lost their jobs. Some work part-time, but don't earn enough to pay the rent on a house or apartment. One American account described the ordeal of a family living in a car at a Californian campsite. They had four children, the father worked in a factory during the day and the mother worked in a fast-food restaurant at night. The parents made $30 a month too much to get welfare assistance, but it wasn't enough to pay the rent. They were told if they continued to keep their children in a car, the children would be taken away from them by social services.

Unemployment

Unemployment causes, or worsens, financial problems in families. Only about 20 percent of the heads of homeless households in Britain and the United States have a job. The 1990 United States National Commission on Children found that the poorest children came from one-parent families without jobs. The report, which concentrates on child poverty, found that in 1987 the poverty rate among black children was 45 percent, among Hispanic children 39 percent, and among whites 15 percent.

More homes needed

Some people blame rising homelessness among families on social trends; they argue that the increase in the breakup of relationships and marriages is one of the causes of the growing numbers of homeless people. This is a popular argument among government or state officials. They claim that where previously a family lived together as one household, now there is a greater likelihood of the same number of people needing two homes if their relationship founders. Generally, there is an increase in the number of households nationally, partly due to divorce and separation, but also because many couples now in their 20s want to set up homes of their own.

Bad for your health

Numerous surveys indicate that health problems are far more common among homeless people than among other groups within the community. Homeless women are three times more likely to be admitted to a hospital during a pregnancy than other women. Many babies born to women who live in temporary housing are of a lower birth weight than children born to other mothers. Both mothers and children are more likely to suffer from various health problems caused by poor sanitation and inadequate diet. These problems of ill health are directly associated with the living conditions – it's hard to keep up a good diet if the kitchen is far away or if there is no adequate space to store food. Many parents who live in shelters or welfare hotels suffer from depression, anxiety, and insomnia.

"**Where we live there is only one stove and that's to share between six families. I hardly ever make the kids hot food. By the time I've carried the plates upstairs it's cold anyway.**" Mother of children aged 5, 7 and 11, in temporary housing.

Safety in the home

Many women living in hotels are concerned about personal safety and feel vulnerable. The building may be without a working elevator so that the access to upper-story rooms is by a lonely staircase. In the United States many of the welfare hotels are in the most violent parts of town, and residents risk being mugged or raped; the hotels themselves are frequently crime-ridden, with drug-dealing, prostitution and muggings.

Many hotels don't have decent kitchens. There may also be too few bathrooms, and a hot water supply that doesn't work properly. Some of the buildings are damp or infested with fleas, mice or rats.

Homeless children

Perhaps homeless children suffer most from living in temporary housing. The housing is often unsuitable, with rooms away from any play space.

Conditions are overcrowded, with inadequate cooking facilities and heating. Thousands of babies live the first years of their lives in cramped conditions and there is little or no privacy for anyone. Because some families may stay in such accommodation for years, relationships between parents and children are under severe stress and often deteriorate.

> **"An estimated 100,000 children are homeless throughout the United States."** Findings of the U.S. National Commission on Children, published in 1990.

Unsuitable housing conditions often interfere with a child's development and behavior. Hotel children are more likely to be later walkers and talkers than other children of the same age. A cramped environment discourages children from learning to walk. The boredom and isolation of spending all day in one room can easily depress mothers, who then do not stimulate their children. They in turn become bored and isolated.

Despite the undoubted ill-effects of living in temporary housing, some people deny that these children are homeless. They claim that because the children have a roof over their heads they should not be classed as homeless.

Hostel life
Hostels, or shelters, also provide temporary accommodation for homeless families, but only for a minority. Many hostels are far pleasanter places than welfare or "bed and breakfast" hotels, and

they are usually run by charities with the help of official funds. As they are staffed they offer families more support and the company of others in similar situations. The staff can sometimes help with finding permanent housing solutions too.

"Both me and my son are sick and life in the hostel doesn't help. There's a lot of support here from other women but I can't stay forever. What I really want is a place of my own." Shirley, staying in a hostel for single parents.

Attitudes toward homeless people
The situation and feelings of homeless families are made worse by the prejudice many have to face. In Britain and in the United States black people make up a disproportionate number of those who are counted as homeless; evidence suggests that they are temporarily housed in the worst conditions and tend to spend longer there.

"People are always saying it's black people that cause the problems. It's not true, but it makes it harder to ask for help. I've enough to cope with without having to put up with some racist housing official."

Women who head households also face discrimination, and there are cases of landlords intimidating and threatening women. As well as the problems of racism and sexism, some families are stigmatized and labeled "problem families," and are blamed for their situation. This makes it

Many homeless families, like this woman and her child, live in "bed and breakfast" accommodation. About 20 percent of families become homeless as a result of a breakdown of marriage or other partnerships.

easier for the authorities to dismiss the families' predicament, rather than try to help.

Uncertainty about the future

The high levels of stress and illness which homeless families, especially women within them, suffer are made worse by an overwhelming uncertainty about the future. Many women feel dumped and abandoned by the authorities and feel they are not properly informed about when they may be rehoused. Women say that this uncertainty is one of the worst aspects of being homeless. It prevents a family from planning ahead, it hinders children from settling in at school, and makes people more reluctant to try and find a job.

CASE STUDY

When Steve, Kerry and their two children were found temporary housing, their first reaction was relief. But now they've been living in cramped conditions for a year and, with no promise of a permanent home, they feel they've been dumped by the authorities.

"I suppose ours is a fairly common story," said Steve.

"It wasn't just one thing that went wrong, but more or less everything at the same time. We've always struggled a bit with money, but when I lost my job at the warehouse, things got out of hand. Kerry was still going out to work part-time and I used some of my unemployment money to keep up with payments, so we weren't broke. But somehow we kept on spending. Not huge amounts of money – but enough to run up a few debts. Then Kerry's mom got sick and Kerry gave up her job to look after her.

"When her mom died Kerry withdrew for months afterward – she couldn't get over it. All the problems seemed to get to her and she started to stay indoors. Well, we fell behind with the rent. When the landlord evicted us, we accepted this temporary place even though we knew it was unsuitable – it's miles away from our old apartment and the kids have to travel a long distance to school. Just paying their bus fares is a problem, but it's a blessing they're old enough to go to school.

"Living here on top of each other, both at home all day, is sheer hell. It's our relationship that takes the strain. I keep looking for another job, sometimes just to get out, but most aren't worth it – I'd end up paying all the rent out of my wages without welfare help. And anyway, when we don't know how long we'll be here, what's the point? We might end up living on the other side of town. I'm worried about leaving Kerry here too – she doesn't feel safe on her own and still feels depressed.

"Conditions here are disgusting. There's not enough hot water, and sometimes you even end up getting in line to go to the toilet. We do our cooking on a stove out in the corridor. I bet if the fire department knew about it, they'd close the place down."

CHAPTER 3

SLEEPING ROUGH – THE ROOFLESS

Homelessness in Britain is growing most quickly among young people. They don't have enough money and there isn't enough housing they can afford to live in.

Single homeless adults are among the most vulnerable and isolated people in society. No one knows how many are "roofless" but their numbers make them a visible presence in the inner cities. Those who have lived on the streets for years may be so broken down that they exist beyond the help of family or friends. They are completely isolated; many do not even claim the welfare benefits to which they are entitled. In Britain about half of the people camping on the streets are mentally ill; many others are young – between 16 and 18 years old. In the United States there is the added problem of increasing numbers of homeless people on the streets who are drug or alcohol users.

"We don't want to be here – don't believe anyone who says we live like this because we want to." Richard, sleeping on the street.

A lifetime of problems

Most of the people who live on the streets have suffered years of setbacks. A deprived family background, problems with education, bad health, unemployment, and low income are common experiences of single homeless people.

The homeless on the streets have tragic stories to tell. They have lost their jobs, suffered family crises; they struggle with alcohol problems, and depression. These misfortunes can cause the collapse of individuals' personal lives, isolating them further and further from social relations until they are adrift on the street. One report on the homeless in London claimed that over half of the younger people had grown up in foster homes.

"Our experience is that the notion of sleeping rough being a chosen life-style is rubbish, and that well-managed shelters attract 'self-referrals' within a few weeks of opening." British housing charity report, 1990.

The stereotypes

Despite all the evidence to the contrary, some people persist in believing that homelessness is caused by irresponsible behavior. The stereotype of single, homeless people depicts them as lazy, unwilling to work or "settle down;" they are seen as the "undeserving poor" who could sort out their problems if only they put their minds to it and stopped being "rootless." Such stereotypes hinder

In New York, the American city with the worst homelessness crisis, many people survive by begging wherever they find a pitch – on street corners or on the subway.

the fight against homelessness because they prevent adequate resources from being allocated to homeless people. They also mask the fundamental causes of homelessness – poverty and the lack of affordable housing.

The stereotypes of the irresponsible, homeless teenager on the street or the out-of-control alcoholic are simply untrue, although there *is* more mental illness, drug use, and alcoholism among homeless people than among the population at large. (One survey in Britain found 13 percent drank heavily and about half those living on the streets have problems of mental health.)

In the United States 44 percent are estimated to be substance abusers (users of drugs or alcohol). In Washington D.C. a random sampling of more than 400 shelter residents found that about 15 percent had used the cocaine-based drug crack within the previous month.

Living on the streets

"**I do go stealing, I have to admit, just to survive. A friend of mine stole a package of cookies and ended up getting three months in prison.**" David, homeless in London.

Sleeping on the streets means you have to be ingenious just to survive. Life on the street is a daily battle to keep warm and find enough to eat. It leaves no time for anything else. Raiding the garbage cans at the back of restaurants to scavenge for food, making a cup of coffee last in a diner, warming up in a laundromat before being told to get out are all ways of getting by.

People sleeping on the streets are more likely to suffer from pneumonia and bronchitis. Yet some homeless people are reluctant to seek medical help when necessary because they think that doctors will be unwilling to treat them. In Britain, some don't even know that they have a right to treatment under the National Health Service. Consequently, single, homeless people are more likely to use accident or emergency services and wait until their illness is serious before seeking help.

Living in a hostel

Hostels, or shelters for single homeless people are a first step away from sleeping on the streets. The

None of the problems of homelessness are new. This illustration shows a kitchen in a London lodging house for homeless people in 1910.

most basic shelters and large-intake hostels offer food, a bed, and access to medical help. Homeless people can come to these "direct access" hostels from the street (hence the name). They are always full and have to turn thousands of people away each year. This type of hostel accommodation is available more to men than women.

However, in some of the big cities in the United States, many people would rather camp on the streets than sleep in the city shelters which are often violent places. The largest city shelters sleep hundreds of people in one room and overcrowded conditions breed violent crimes such as knifings, beatings and muggings.

In Britain and the United States many smaller "direct access hostels" are run by charities aided by official funds. Pine Street Inn in Boston is run by state and voluntary contributions. Every night it provides shelter for 500 men and 50 women on a first-come first-served basis. During the winter extra guests are allowed to sleep on the floor rather than be turned away into the freezing cold.

> "I've been sleeping in the cabs of big trucks waiting in the yard to be sold, but you've got to get away early or they have the police on you. When you wake up, you realize you have got to get back out there in the cold and the days are just depressing."

Substantial numbers of the people adrift on the streets come from institutionalized backgrounds; they have grown up in foster homes, joined the army perhaps, and never had a stable home. Lack of basic social skills contributes to their isolation. Specialized hostels for the single homeless often teach social and employment skills and aim to improve individuals' capacity for self-sufficiency in the hope that they will eventually resettle in the community. Some hostels offer programs to help with drug or alcohol addiction, and all offer a more secure environment.

> **"You can watch TV and talk to everyone. I've been living on the streets for the last ten years. I don't come to the shelter that often, just when I need the company."** Adam, aged 55.

Some bizarre arrangements are made for the homeless. In one program in New York, homeless people sleep overnight in shelters out in the suburbs. Every morning buses transport hundreds of these homeless back to the city to beg. This arrangement costs the New York administration $1,000 a month per person – the price of renting a one-bedroom apartment in the city.

The problems of some single homeless people make them difficult to approach. They can be aggressive, out of touch on drugs, drunk, or incoherent. Some single homeless exist beyond the social net and they have become isolated. As part of the fight against homelessness some workers take to the streets to contact these people who live out in the cold.

Stay at home – young homeless
In a situation where there is less cheap housing to

rent, young people are increasingly at risk of becoming homeless. They are last in line when it comes to allocating low-income housing. Yet young people need temporary accommodation. Increasingly the British government takes the attitude that young people should stay at home until they are financially independent. For many, this is asking the impossible. Many of the young people who become homeless have grown up in foster homes and have never had a family home of their own. Others have lost their home on the death of their parents, or sometimes parents have separated, so the home is no longer open to the children. Often, the home may simply be intolerable because of domestic violence or abuse.

"When my dad was in one of his 'moods,' he just went for me. He'd lash out and it always seemed to be me he picked on. As soon as I could I left; I went to stay on a friend's floor but she got tired of me being around and asked me to go. Now I'm staying in this hostel." Sally, aged 17.

The British government's stay-at-home attitude is reflected in recent social security changes, and these are a major cause of the increase in homelessness among young people in Britain. Money which was paid out for board and lodgings has been cut back for those under 26 years of age, leaving many with no real housing options.

The big city

Some young people move to the larger cities – they

hope to find a job, companionship, and excitement. They arrive on the streets with only the clothes they wear and no money. If they don't find a job immediately they risk ending up homeless. Major cities like London act as a magnet for these people; one study found that four-fifths of young people at a night shelter were from outside the capital and had arrived recently from areas of high unemployment. But generally most young homeless people remain within a few miles of where they grew up. As a result, homelessness is not only an inner city phenomenon – provincial towns and rural areas also share the problem.

Some young people leave home without adequate planning or resources, perhaps as part of their struggle for independence. They think life on the streets looks good – from a distance it might. They see teenagers who are well dressed in the latest fashions and with money. To someone stuck in appalling conditions at home, these street kids look glamorous. However, their money is earned through prostitution, or petty dealing in drugs and crime. These teenagers gamble with their safety and health. They look good one week, but are beaten up the next.

> **"I've never felt I had a home and I don't expect to have one. I left foster care and went into a shelter. The past two years I've worked as a prostitute. People say it's degrading, but it's not as bad as having no money at all."** Kelly, aged 20.

CHAPTER 4

MENTAL HEALTH

This woman lives on the street with her possessions wrapped in bags. In the United States many homeless people – especially those who are mentally ill – prefer the streets to city shelters where they risk victimization from other residents.

Mentally ill people form a significant element of the new homeless. Their number has greatly increased in recent years. Why has this change occurred? In industrialized countries – especially the United States, Britain, Italy, and Portugal – since the 1950s there has been a strong movement arguing for the care of the mentally ill in the community. This movement reacted to the fact that many people were being kept in hospitals or asylums unnecessarily, who could, with adequate provision, be cared for in the community.

In principle, everyone agreed with this, however the antiasylum lobby argued that as asylums were not needed they should all be closed down. This lobby also assumed that adequate funds would be available to provide care in the community. This has not been the case. During the past ten years 23,000 psychiatric beds have been closed, which leaves thousands of people on the streets without adequate care. In the United States there are approximately 500,000 fewer patients in mental hospitals today than in the mid-1950s, when the numbers living in institutions peaked at 650,000.

"On a bad day I don't care whether I'm alive or dead. Anyway no one notices what happens to me. I drink to make myself feel better. Friends – what's a friend? I feel I've been on my own all my life, though sometimes I can get close to others out on the street." Mary, aged 40, who has lived in the streets for the last year since leaving the hospital where she was treated for depression.

Slipping through the net

Community care still remains the favored option of most mental health workers, but it is expensive and usually underfunded. Today, community care can be inadequate care, and so disturbed people do not get the treatment they need. All too often they slip through the net of social services and end up on the street. When their illness goes untreated, their condition deteriorates, causing them even greater distress. One survey in London found that 44 percent of the destitute people interviewed were psychotic (a severe derangement of the personality which may make a person out of touch with reality), and a further 16 percent had been discharged from psychiatric hospitals after treatment for psychoses. The survey pointed out that these people were extremely withdrawn and isolated, without friends or acquaintances. The same survey found that more than 90 percent had "migrated to London from elsewhere." In California and New York where the situation is worse, two out of every five people who are suffering from psychoses do not receive any treatment.

> **"Huge numbers of psychotic people are struggling to survive outside hospital, with dwindling support from social services, often none whatsoever."** Study of destitute people in London, published 1989.

The need for asylum

In the enthusiasm for community care, the needs of the chronically mentally ill have been eclipsed. Many of these people can be better cared for in an asylum, and there is a growing lobby of psychiatrists and social workers who are calling for a few asylums to remain open to look after people with long-term mental health problems.

> "I didn't want to leave hospital but I had to. I'd lived there for 20 years. Mind you, I remember I didn't want to go into hospital in the first place. Where I live now is alright – the landlady helps me get on – but before coming here I'd slept rough and lived in a couple of hostels."
> James, diagnosed as schizophrenic.

The closure of the larger psychiatric hospitals coincides with a cutting back generally of hospital beds for mentally ill people. Increasingly, the hospitals are only geared to short stays, yet chronic mental ill health can last a lifetime.

> "It's a cycle. They're homeless so they can't cope and they come into hospital; they leave but there's no help so they go back on the street and can't cope and it starts again."
> Psychiatrist.

Changing one institution for another
Some of the people who lived in psychiatric hospitals, and who should be cared for in the community, end up in prisons. They are usually sentenced for petty crimes such as theft or perhaps disorderly behavior on the streets. The presence of large numbers of mentally distressed people in prisons adds to the tensions already erupting in

these overcrowded institutions. One institution is being exchanged for another with inappropriate facilities. In prison, mentally ill people may not get all the treatment they need, and the risk of suicide is high. Ironically, the British government plans to close 77 hospitals – and open 26 new prisons, including one on the site of a recently closed psychiatric hospital. In fact the cost of keeping a person prisoner is generally higher than paying for a bed in a psychiatric hospital.

> **"I go stealing. The way I look at it – it's survival, improving my standard of living. And then I get caught. Sometimes I'm homeless, sometimes in prison or hospital. I don't know which is worse."**

Resettlement and rehabilitation

Many single homeless people with mental health problems come to the large-intake hostels and shelters. From there they may move to hostels which provide more specialized care. In the United States, the Netherlands, Denmark, and Canada, a new type of hostel, called a clubhouse, offers an alternative to some expsychiatric patients. The clubhouse works on a membership system; every member is responsible for a specific task, from peeling potatoes to shopping or cooking the meal. Every task performed is appreciated and rewarded. This makes for a therapeutic environment in which the clubhouse members' contributions are always valued. Eventually, members take on work outside the clubhouse. However, if a member is too ill to work, one of the clubhouse staff will stand in for him or her. This means that clubhouse members can be more confident that they can keep their jobs without worrying that days off due to illness will result in getting the sack, and employers can rely on the job being done.

Research shows that the clubhouse model provides an environment that helps to rehabilitate expsychiatric patients. Membership in the clubhouse is for life and there is evidence that members need fewer readmissions to hospitals for treatment. The first clubhouse in Britain is to be opened by an innovative charity which works with single homeless people. In the United States, 200 clubhouses already offer help to young homeless people. It's an expensive option – but it works.

In Britain and the United States the amount of money spent on building low-income housing has been cut back. Children from poor families and the mentally ill are among the first to suffer.

CASE STUDY

Lynn has been diagnosed schizophrenic several times. She's 31 and has spent a lot of her adult life in psychiatric hospitals. She grew up in a violent home, and she and her sister spent long periods in foster care. Lynn went to college, but had a breakdown. She feels she has never recovered from that and agrees she needs a lot of support.

"My sister helps me a lot. She's been really good to me and stuck by me. I've moved here to live closer to her but it's been an uphill struggle to get an apartment in this area, even with the help of a sympathetic psychiatrist and social worker.

"Before I moved here, I was staying at this hostel. I was there for three years and then got the message to leave once I was improving. I was supposed to manage in this bed and breakfast place but I knew I couldn't handle that."

Lynn's condition got worse. She stopped taking the medication she needed and became more distressed. Eventually she was picked up wandering the streets – five months pregnant. She'd been living on the streets for a couple of weeks.

No one really knew where to place Lynn; none of the psychiatric hospitals wanted to admit her and considered her main problem to be lack of suitable housing. At this point her parents accepted her back into their home, but once the baby was a few months old, family tensions erupted again and Lynn and her baby left to stay in a hostel. From there she eventually moved to the apartments near her sister's.

"I kept saying to everyone I just needed some time to sort myself out and a place of my own."

In Lynn's case illness came before homelessness, but often it's impossible to know which comes first. The pressures of homelessness make illness worse. On the other hand, psychiatric illness can cause homelessness, loss of a job, and the breakdown of family support, because people find it difficult to live and work with the mentally ill.

CHAPTER 5

THE FIGHT AGAINST HOMELESSNESS

Charities and volunteers help to ease the plight of the homeless. "Crisis at Christmas" offers a square meal on the day most people expect to be at home with their families eating plenty.

The size of the homelessness problem has shocked both governments and the public into action. But will the focus on homelessness continue for long enough to make an impact on policymakers? Countries like Britain and the United States require changes in policy to increase government spending on housing.

Public expenditure on housing

Many countries allocate a proportion of their national income to the cost of building houses. Denmark, West Germany, and France are among the highest spenders, and maintain policies that provide low-income housing at affordable rents. Britain is amongst the lowest spenders and allocates an even smaller proportion of its national income on housing than less wealthy countries like Portugal or Ireland.

Lower spending in itself need not be a problem if the amount and condition of the housing available is adequate. But as people have been encouraged to buy the public housing they occupy, a lot of the better low-income housing has been sold. The result has been the lowering of the amount and standard of the remaining housing. Some is unfit for habitation and stands empty for want of money to pay for repairs.

"This estate used to be alright, but not anymore. Some people own their own houses and others don't. We used to all get along – now there's a them and us." Sheila, who lives on a subsidized housing estate in Birmingham, England.

Building new houses

During World War II many large European cities were badly bombed and millions of homes were destroyed. When the war ended and the soldiers returned to civilian life, there was an acute housing shortage. By the 1950s an extensive building program was underway. These building programs provided employment. But supply never kept pace with demand, especially when the number of households increased. In Britain, waiting lists for subsidized housing grew, yet there was a dramatic reduction in housing planned and built by local authorities (of 85 percent between the mid-1970s and 1991). Today Britain is short of at least one million new homes.

Some low-income houses, like this one in the north of England, are damp or in need of repair. But the majority of low-income house tenants are satisfied with their houses – complaints are usually against private landlords.

"It is social rented housing which is required – it's no good the private sector increasing its level of housebuilding when the groups who are most at risk of homelessness face that risk because they can't compete in the owner-occupier market." Housing researcher, 1990.

Using empty buildings

Look around any city and you'll see a number of buildings standing empty. Some charities want these sites to be used as temporary shelters in a low-cost attempt to tackle homelessness. During a cold period in London, a charity for the homeless was paid by the government health department to provide temporary shelter. Mattresses were put on the floor of a disused hospital and shelter was offered for four days. After that the government department considered the cold weather to be over and most of the people were returned to the streets. The mattresses remained in place.

"What is so frustrating is that we know what the solutions are. If there were places in hostels, they wouldn't stay on the streets. We just don't have the resources." Housing charity worker.

This type of "direct access" accommodation in disused hospitals or schools could offer homeless people somewhere to sleep other than the streets. Some empty residential housing could also be brought back into use to provide homes for those currently without; after all, most people staying in shelters would prefer to live in ordinary self-contained and permanent homes.

Prevention of homelessness

Building programs are expensive, but there are other ways of beginning to tackle the homelessness problem which don't require massive funds. Groups most at risk, such as children leaving care, single women enduring, or threatened with, physical or sexual abuse, could be identified and rehoused as a priority.

Since not keeping up with the mortgage repayments or falling behind with the rent lead to homelessness, debt counseling could assist people who are in arrears. This would help families manage their affairs and so reduce the risk of them losing their homes.

Health care

Health care should be made more accessible to homeless people. Some are unaware of their right to medical help; doctors need to advertise these rights to improve access. Other people who are in contact with homeless people need to know more about the problems they face. For example, teachers need to understand the domestic problems faced by homeless children.

Accepting the problem

In many ways it is easier to assume that people are homeless simply through their own choice. That way the state is not responsible for their plight and is therefore under less obligation to provide relief. In some towns, such as Phoenix, Arizona, the

The increase in owner occupation, and a decrease in public and low-rent housing have led to the homelessness crisis. Here apartments built as low-income housing are for sale under the British government's right to buy scheme.

attitude that the homeless are to blame has allowed the authorities to avoid making any provision for fear it might encourage them. These authorities persist in seeing homeless people as bums to be run out of town. So people are forced to live in tents or cars, but risk being moved on or prosecuted under strict trespassing laws. In Britain, people are increasingly fined for begging in the streets or charged under an outdated vagrancy act. This is a form of harassment of homeless people, and ignores their fundamental problems. Homeless people exist with very few rights; without an address they can't vote, nor can they receive welfare or social security benefits. Many legal changes are required to improve their position.

Raising money

Although governments have the primary financial responsibility toward the homeless, many charities provide facilities which are paid for by donations and by a combination of state and private funds. Some charities have novel fund-raising events; for example, National Sleep Out Week which is held in Britain every year asks people to sleep outside for one night – in their school, office or garden – with only a cardboard box for shelter. The people sleeping outside get a glimpse of what it's like to sleep rough and, because they ask friends to sponsor them, they also raise money to help the homeless.

Private companies can donate money to charities who work with homeless people in the inner cities. Perhaps people are sleeping in the street entrance to their offices?

A safe home

Everyone who has a safe and secure home knows how important it is. Yet it is a basic right denied to millions of people throughout the world. Although voluntary workers and charities can provide food and shelter for the night, only governments can provide permanent housing for the homeless. One British housing charity, Shelter, which has been campaigning on the behalf of homeless people for the past 20 years, emphasizes the fact that homelessness is a problem that shames affluent societies: "The basic message remains the same. In a truly civilized society, nothing less than a secure and decent home for all will do."

SOURCES OF HELP

There are organizations which offer counseling about problems at home and advice to young people in housing need:

The Association to Benefit Children
316 East 88th Street
New York, New York 10128

Department of Health and Human Services
Community Services/Family Assistance
370 L'Enfant Promenade, S.W.
Washington, D.C. 20447

Housing Assistance Council
1025 Vermont Avenue, N.W.
Suite 606
Washington, D.C. 20005

National Coalition for the Homeless
105 East 22nd Street
New York, New York 10010

National Federation of Housing Counselors
2706 Ontario Road, N.W.
Washington, D.C. 20009

Partnership for the Homeless
115 West 31st Street
New York, New York 10001-2109

There are also a number of books on the subject, such as the selection listed below, which may provide further information and advice.

Beckelman, Laurie. *Homeless*. New York: Crestwood House, 1989.

Burch, Claire. *Homeless in the Eighties*. Regent Press, 1989.

Hyde, Margaret O. *Homeless: Profiling the Problem*. Enslow Pubs., 1989.

Kosof, Anna. *Homeless in America*. Franklin Watts, 1988.

Landau, Elaine. *Homeless*. Messner, 1987.

O'Connor, Karen. *Homeless Children*. Lucent Books, 1989.

Thorman, George. *Homeless Families*. C.C. Thomas, 1988.

WHAT THE WORDS MEAN

"bed and breakfast" In Britain many families are temporarily housed in cheap hotels, which, despite their name, rarely provide breakfast. Nearly all bed and breakfast housing is of a poor standard.

direct access hostels are open to anyone from off the street. They provide a bed for the night and food. Many are large, with beds arranged in open dormitories. Usually the guests have to leave the hostel during the day.

low-income housing is the name given to social housing. Federal government finances building the housing which is then sold to private landlords who let it to tenants at lower rents for a fixed term.

mortgage Most houses in America are bought with the help of a mortgage – money which is lent from a bank or building society toward the cost of buying the house. The money-lender then owns a share of the house. Mortgages are paid back over an agreed number of years and with interest. Falling behind with mortgage repayments can lead to homelessness if the bank repossesses the house.

private rented sector refers to housing owned by private landlords which is then rented to tenants. Increasingly, most housing in the private rented sector is intended for high-income people and let for high rents.

social housing is housing built for people who cannot afford to buy their own homes. Usually it is financed by local or national government. In Britain it is called council housing and in the United States low-income housing.

subsidy is a grant of money paid by the government to keep costs down.

tenure is the way in which the right to occupy property is held. In the past most people had the right to live in their home because they paid rent. Today, owning the home is the mass tenure; increasingly people have the right to live in their homes because they own them.

Index

Photographic credits

Cover: Roger Vlitos; pages 4, 13, 16, 26, 29, 33, 36, 40, 42, 44, 46, 49, 51, 52 and 54: Marie-Helene Bradley; page 10: The *Daily Telegraph* Newspaper; pages 21 an 31: J. Allan Cash Library; page 23: Vaness Bailey.